SOAP

SOAP

CHARLOTTE GUEST

Soap
Recent Work Press
Canberra, Australia

Copyright © Charlotte Guest 2017

National Library of Australia
Cataloguing-in-Publication entry.
Guest, Charlotte
Soap/ Charlotte Guest

ISBN: 9780648087816 (paperback)

All rights reserved. This book is copyright. Except for private study, research, criticism or reviews as permitted under the Copyright Act, no part of this book may be reproduced, stored in a retrieval system, or transmitted in any form by any means without prior written permission. Enquiries should be addressed to the publisher.

Cover design: Recent Work Press
Set in Bembo by Recent Work Press

recentworkpress.com

*for mum and dad
and Gabby*

Contents

Harvest	1
Networking Drinks	2
Egg Tempera	3
Hush, Memory	4
Baskets	5
Picnic at the Rock	7
For Eurydice	8
Hey Sweetheart, Hey Love	9
Bivouac	10
From Page 144 of a Seminal Text	11
Goodfellas	12
Hey Preacher	13
Midnight	14
Blue Days	16
Great Knot	17
From Everything to Air	18
Autobiographical Fragment	19
Birds for Love	21
Elegies for Oceans	22
Pleistocene Soup	24
Summer Doors	26
Things that have weight/Must exist	27
Nanna, Kalamunda	28
Daddies	29
Summer Nude	30
Katharine	31
The Seagull	32
Barnacles	33
Love Poem	34
Notes on the Disappearance of a Friend	37
Afterword	44

Is anyone ever ready for exactly who they are?

Fay Zwicky

Harvest

The strongest women on earth farm
the cassava. They sing
the root from the ground
against empty bellies and the prospect
of rot.
    Cultivated in circles five
    thousand years wide
    like the coastless Sargasso.

Time magazine warns
that when prepared incorrectly,
the root produces cyanide,
and some will be allergic
regardless.
    Cultivated in circles five
    thousand years wide
    like the coastless Sargasso.

We are advised to opt
for a different dessert.

Networking Drinks

'You see society through old
frames, you are perpetuating that
against which you argue,'
says a confident boy with flushed
capillaries, exalting in this
repartee. 'No, what I am saying is,
the historically oppressed
form allegiances based
on the common ground of dis-
advantage.' I
hold my gaze. His eyes bulge
as he takes a swig from
his Old Fashioned, looking
down his straight nose
at me. 'Why are we still
bandying about old terms?
Why do we still talk
of race and gender?
Have the last fifty years
meant nothing?'
I open my mouth and
push bubbles out.
We are talking
underwater, sacks
over our heads, like
dipped witches.

Egg Tempera

A grinding in your stomach, deeply felt,
beneath the fleshy dunes your mother said
would have been considered beautiful
in the late 1400s.
                              You rise and fall
as the bars on your lover's stereo.
He hitches your wool skirt and ignores
the tears that tour your face and make you
think of your Renaissance sisters,
stroked into existence.
                                     We girls,
we bleeding, breathless girls, taking
dumb solace in the fact our bodies
have a long history, are politically charged,
and would've been considered beautiful
in the late 1400s.
                              When it's over
you roll onto your stomach, inspect yourself
with a period eye, and look to the site
marked by tepid blots.

Hush, Memory

The lodgings at the end of girlhood
are not as advertised. I had not expected
these island features, or the grass
to whip. I wasn't told hard rubbish
would run all month. Our doors are
red; our mirrors done over with breath.

It seems I have forgotten all I learnt
at Revolution School, and instead glide
past Neptune Pools in a car I do not own.
I go for walks; I slip company; lock my door
against the nighttime world of dangerous living
and look for peace among my sheets.

The house rests heavily on imagination
and is encircled by a garden in which I sit
and listen to the politics of flowers.
Laughter peels summer air; sometimes
mine, sometimes far-off women.
Here, the trees speak. Here, the rooms
are as mouths with opinions, their beds
loose tongues. There is no end to the opinions
of rooms. Some of us didn't make it to the lodgings
at the end of girlhood. Some will climb
the front steps as if to a monument.
The tops of flowers nod like many girlish faces,
and, when the wind changes,
begin to shake.

Baskets

There is
a sense of walking
with dreams and
uneasy things
in my arms, like
groceries purchased
at closing. Forever
pounding
the supermarket's
sliding doors
as 'there's just one
more thing I need'.
Security leads me
to the necessities aisle
where girls in green shirts
are restocking. They
fill my basket with
things I know I
have at home.
My groceries change
shape, become things
I didn't want to buy.
They roll like ornaments
in a ship's cabin;
I am a captain
used to smaller vessels.
I ask my groceries what
they are doing, changing like
that. They roll out my door and
under cars and throw
themselves in bins.

There is a
garbage smell
in the kitchen. The
soy sauce I know
I had is gone. As
is the fruit I thought
I could rely on. And
always, always, a sense
of grey bags splitting
and spilling
and someone
laughing.

Picnic at the Rock

> *What was her name, the tall pale girl with straight yellow hair, who had gone skimming over the water like one of the white swans on his uncle's lake?*
>
> Joan Lindsay, *Picnic at Hanging Rock*

The child ascends a great formation with the idea of catching all the day's light in an empty jar. It is 1999, and the turning is on everyone's lips. Atop the myth and the monolith, the science of the sun conjoins with magic: three floating corsets, warped from 99 years in stills and rushes. *Can you hear the pansies?* The child places the jar and inhales radiance (she must capture the sun's sticky fingers before the earth completes a day's rotation). In time, the corsets swan, and, as if in a dream, the child lends her hand to touch them, and on her fingers she smells the old girls' skin leaking from a hot day in the bush. Then, a chorus softly, *here even the birds do walk.*

For Eurydice

The naturalist amid
her ground-truthing,
turns the sand and
gives it

a knowing look.
Picking her way up
the tan slope, a
bobbing desert bird,

she is attuned to the electric pop
of cicadas
and a sense of wrongness:
the sacrificial giving of

her skin
to the sun.

Hey Sweetheart, Hey Love

I
am a nighttime walker,

I prefer dark, dark public parks,
the sound of the bush
splitting a grin, baked earth
beneath my stalker's feet.

A night time walker, I
prefer outskirts around my
walker's knees, the sound of the silken
breeze.

I, a night time
walker, am a
conduit for remarks.

I am a nighttime walker.
A *matter-of-time* walker. An
it's-awful-but-she banshee
proffering blistering screams.

I—
a *look up* walker, a *lock up*
walker, a parcel of soft
runnels—am gunning my way
home.

Bivouac

The terms of our arrangement
are revised every three days. You
trace my bones, protruding
through my skin, as we
recap the clauses, their causes,
and intended effects. Let's

press together the bodies we live in,
let's let in a modicum of wildness,
select for each other new monikers,
and mine our histories. Let's act out
attentiveness to language, small acts
of understanding, setting all else aside
to erect a shelter under each other's
smells, each other's sounds.

All we want
stitched into
this night, this bed,
these woven fingers.

From Page 144 of a Seminal Text

Imaginations
of
the
strangest
kind:
of cliff
sea
cloud
sky

pools
of
uneasy
water

man
and
woman
and
the
white
earth

remote
pleasures

familiar
virtues

something
alien
to
domestic
life

Goodfellas

You meddle a long time
with the power board
and extension cords, in order
to shed light and clothes
in warmth and comfort. In order
to say *fuck off* to fear. To
scoop up lightness
and offer it
like so many letters home.
You curse at the state of my
electricals, tell me it's a
fire hazard, that we
could have gone up
in our sleep. That we could have
died young and unfulfilled, stopped,
like the rain stops,
and hearts are still.

Hey Preacher

> *Jesus died for somebody's sins but not mine.*
> Patti Smith

Be groovy or leave, man. Bob Dylan in the speakers, holding my hand and God's. I took my velvet coat and slithered into the night. They called me The Confidence Man. I started the car. The machine stroked the road as we glided through the streets, every night 'til 2:00am, dropping angels off at bars. Time was a physical thing then, a thing with three dimensions that stretched on and on like my mother talking. I remember when I took the job, when it occurred to me. I remember thrashing around to Hendrix, watching people look at art. I remember ascending the stairs to his gallery feeling like something was about to happen. There was an atmosphere of brink. He had the fever. He was cold and sweating. I took out a handkerchief and wiped his brow. We hummed together, singing the moment, and then we were silent. You've got a cowboy's mouth, I said. He smiled, and you've got the eyes of a preacher.

Midnight

We laze all day on the back verandah,
watching
the dawn come,
the dawn go,

like an ocean breathing.
Heads swimmy with others' germs,
we compare

white tongues
and pink tonsils.

The noon comes,
the noon goes,

pressing a flat palm to
our bellies, a toddler enquiring
after a coming sibling.

The day bears witness to
our better selves
that might extend into

tomorrow, or not,
that might bedazzle,
or not.

Then, when the sky explodes
I turn to you and ask,
'What are the fireworks for?'

And you say,
'Midnight.'

whe
re is your
secret hiding
place? Who may
go there, and what
are the rules? Is it damp,
is it dark inside? Whose n
ames have you collected in
your secret hiding place, like
medium-sized rocks in a circle
articulating your wild solitude?
Have you arranged things in a d
eliberately absent way, like a wor
k-space flat-lay, or the windswept
look? Are these papers blueprints f
or living? What happened in the act
of hiding? Was it complicated? Do yo
u collapse into the present like colla
psing onto a water-mattress, a water
bed pumped with milk some months
ago? Do you sleep? Do you sleep well
? Do you take the Eucharist and call i
t a 'dinner party' to be both conserva
tive and subversive at the same tim
e? Are you a fraud? Do you live po
litely and write with a sharp ton
gue? Is your cleverness weighi
ng on you like flour that mak
es the stew heavy, and ot
her heavy things? Ar
e you undone? A
re you und
one?

Blue Days

A cygnet was brought in
from the lake,
its neck broken by a
pure bred dog.

I read about the bird.

I heard swan song.

The driveway casts shadows
on my lounge room walls.
I read somewhere

the world itself is residue.

The sound of blood in transit
is oceanic – I am small again,
holding a shell to my ear.

The cygnet was buried;
the dog put to sleep.

Cold stars switch on
at the end of blue days.

Great Knot

Across Nairn Road
she lurches

on a cloudless
Tuesday—

a body full of organs
the weight of wanting—

between green light
and stationary cars.

From Everything to Air

The journalist shuffles down William Street unaware of the sun. The archivist, crossing the boulevard, closes her eyes and imagines scenes on the other side of skin. In the café, the analyst sets his glasses aside to look through the window at a disappeared world. The grocer casts a glance into the river, sinking his thoughts into its silky bosom, and wonders at his run of bad luck. The children toss their hoops.

Autobiographical Fragment

                    The blue balloons,
inflated to the size of modest goals,
like regular pay, attract people, as
flowers attract bees. They are involved
in the world of invisible forces.

                    It is a birthday party.
I watch from the window opposite.
Nearly-women and nearly-men arrive
and disappear into the pumping heart
of the apartment.

                    Suddenly, I am transported
back to Rachel's eighteenth birthday:
we held a funeral for her youth. We
buried a doll in a shoebox lined with
Eucalyptus tissues. The doll
stared into middle distance
all the way down.

                    After the grave was
sealed, Rachel emerged from behind
the shed to effervescent music.
She was draped in a white sheet,
a smudge of light growing slowly nearer,
like death from the perspective of the
dying. Her feet arched and fell; her toes
transformed into gentle animals nosing
the ground. We reached for her

                    through affected tears
and stifled giggles. She was our messiah:
older than the rest of us, schooled in
the secrets of Eros and Thanatos. She
passed cryptic notes in chemistry:
*Everyone who loves should spend time
with the periodic table.*

            Who are we
in the places we occupy? The door
to the apartment opposite opens.
A young woman steps out and folds
over the balcony like laundry. She
slides her weight more fully in my
direction, as if to say *I sense here the
limits of my life.*

The air makes a sound
as I suck it through my teeth.

Birds for Love

The couples in this suburb
walk the cemetery

squinting at the undersides
of birds

stretching their necks
up, up,

forming right angles with their
companions, and their

companions' companions,
all the way back to

the enormous years
without animals.

Elegies for Oceans

In this,
a very old part of the world,
the conservationists plot
marine parks—
big cubes of empty blue—
and watch percentiles go up,
go down, an ocean breathing

in a white laboratory.
The fish here
grow slowly and live
a very long time;
spectral shapes move
under the glass-bottomed boat.
It is perpetual
evening. Look:

they have blow-up bellies
that graze the sea-floor,
the sea-floor like the moon,
the moon the place to go next.
But here: many scenes of water.

Bouncing in the car,
hot maps sticking to our
laps. *I see the sea*
and the sea sees me.
Jiggling summer people
on the way to Paradise.
Paradise: into which we run,

and away from which we run,
like stitches. The sun steps down
and brushes the tips of small waves.
And the ocean twinkles.
And the ocean smiles
like a glass raised to good health,

and posterity.

Pleistocene Soup

In the kitchen
I prepare
Pleistocene soup

and watch a program
on big old things
before concrete.

I imagine megabeasts
where we sit, grazing
on a much younger earth,

and the first
modern humans
sharing hot food.

In the news,
a footprint as big
as your trunk

undressed itself
before a sad woman
walking
along the shore.

A sad woman walking
the shore—
observing the primal
rhythms

of the sea, that crept
in its solid way
over mammals' backs

and now
licks her toes
like a terrier—

bent, as I bend to pick up
clothes, wiped, as I wipe
benchtops and mouths,

and touched
millions.

Summer Doors

Summer doors are sea-coloured;
have no end to shapes; are formless,
like things before names; do not know
grief, or wanting, and can be stubborn
in their optimism.
                Summer doors are
plump, a good memory already formed,
a memory in which doors are open, and
we glide like fish: Mum has no shoes, Dad
has no manners.
                The dog is his dumb self,
and dinner is grey meat and beans. The
scraps in the bin attract animals (an air
born correspondence). Summer doors are legs
in commercials.
                Then change creeps up
—that gradual animal—and we all file
inside like solid census data, taking up positions
in the study, the kitchen, participating in the
economy of small tasks.
                We are weightless,
we are light as breath. We are leaning
into a history that speaks in a language
that rolls and bubbles and spits.

**Things that have weight
Must exist**

Falling into a wide and glassy lake,
she catches sight of her body
before smashing through its limits.

She pierces the immense sky,
the infinite clouds.

An airplane makes its way
across the hills and valleys
caused by the collision.

All the world cupped
in an irregular shape.

Nanna, Kalamunda

Lift your arm, *that* arm,
that arm that held my father,
and once held me, and who tends now
to your gooseflesh and eyes, black tea.

Foot *out,* out the black shoe,
the shoe you think you
went to town in, but really
did a turn about the room.

Open your mouth, your mouth of
fat stories carried off on
someone else's lips—mine, my father's—
your mouth of surface breathing,

your mouth of your eyes,
your mouth of eighty years,
that reeks of love.

We love you, love you Nanna
We wait wait wait
for you to die, Nanna,
wanting you to die, Nanna,

consider
helping you along.

Daddies

Slumped on the garden step, my father,
his storied hands writ large, is
soothed by the night's coolness and
harangued by images
of bigger moons.

At his hip, the softs of my feet
twitch; my mouth sluices his face
with questions in quick
succession:

What happens if a comet hits the earth tonight?
Where in the world is it tomorrow right now?
Who were you before me?

Perturbed, my father,
says something about skin cells
and every ten years,
meaning I've had four fathers
and am a very lucky girl.

Tell me of the first daddy, and the second daddy, I say,
right up 'til the fourth daddy that had me.
Heavy-lidded, palimpsest skin,
breath the scent of pale fire,
it is suddenly time to eat.

Summer Nude

after Elise Blumann

Does anyone remember
the house? The melaleuca?
There were drooping bodies
in the brilliant light; blanched
children disappearing into sand;
and unnameable shapes. A figure
emerged to new life from the river,
stopped in a classic contrapposto pose.
I could see from my window Botticelli
on the Swan. There was no reason
for nakedness except the white hot thrill
of being truly themselves.

Merry bands of colour
expressed in only a few lines.

Katharine

A fragile sequence of
unlikelies, delivers you
at the paneless window.

Propped as the face that sits
in the fingernail moon,
you chortle with the magpies

and observe the folding
of visions.

Here, silence means
the scribble of lorikeets,
the murmur of bees,

the percussive scrub,
and the beat
of nodding flora.

As Apollo drags his burden
through the sky,
you wonder at God

tucked up in the undergrowth
fingers in his ears
sleeping through

anvil clashes
and pellets
slicing the air.

The Seagull

At university I studied a bad poem, bad in the opinion of T S Eliot. The images don't build upon each other in a meaningful way, he wrote, and there is no continuity of thought. He had similar theories about the canon: each work added should rearrange those that precede it. The poem we studied progresses through the parts of a ship, charting the visions of someone drowning, until suddenly a seagull splices the lines and drops heavily onto its internal harmonies, clanging like a bung chord. *Fucking bird, the brazenness of it*, said Eliot, as if a good poem resists the accidents of moments, or ignores the fact we are not at peace inside. As if a good poem is only symmetry, only grace and music, defining itself against the day's apparel. As if a seagull would not split a man's sight of the ship from which he fell. As if it would wait for the man to go under. As if it would care. As if the bird cares for poetry that cannot be flown through.

Barnacles

The plastic shipwreck we bought
for its garishness, its smallness,
because it never sailed anyone anywhere,
is growing barnacles.

No matter the scooping
of our small ocean,
or the cleaning of the tank,
the water undoes itself

and reveals barnacles.

I begin seeing barnacles
in the shower, up the walls

and in the fruit we bought
at market. We begin zoning
the wet areas and quarantine

ourselves. Barnacles fill our mouths and
creep along our legs, drinking
the floods inside us.

We can no longer stand
rough elbows or the blue stains
on our clothes. We cannot drink

salt water. For hours, and hours
a sliding feeling, as
a fish, a big ship
sinking.

Love Poem

1.
One day we will cast
ungenerous glances
at each other's faces,
each other's limbs,
and notice time stamps.

Some days we will not delight.
We will hurt. The suds in the sink
will churn and churn,
beating out the passage of time.
We should prepare for this.

What do you see?
I see the line between date-of-birth
and date-of-death. I see polished granite,
all our ecstasies and hollows stuffed
into an innocuous phrase:
> *Loving wife and mother,* or
> *Loving husband and father.*

2.
I dreamt we donated all our belongings
and became anarchists. Our children's hair
grew wild. We played in the ocean
gulping air between waves, and felt
free. Our adulthoods were spent
as ambassadors of delight.

When I woke I heard your even breathing.
I reached for your hip under the sheets
and stroked your skin – smooth,
as if worked over by waves for millennia.
Smooth, like I could stand

on the shore with my jeans rolled up,
feet numb from the cold, and skip you,
watch you lunge, and lunge, and disappear.

Notes on
the Disappearance
of a Friend

In time, it becomes bearable:
this is the most unbearable part.

Time pushes you along like a celestial wind;

or you sit with your knees under your chin
in a boat on an indigo sea.

Everything is upside down,
like sunlight coming through floorboards,

like lowering food to your mouth.

Silver memories—accents on a calm harbor—
are too bright to look at.

Afterword

Like many poetry collections, *Soap* is a very personal document. It circles around notions of self and belonging, and questions of femininity and feminism. *Soap* is both an interrogation and celebration of private worlds, my private world.

Writing this collection has been as much about the process as about the poems. It has been an exercise in being alone and feeling at ease. It is about, and the result of, solitude. I wrote these poems over a period of six years, from ages nineteen to twenty-five, and so *Soap* also charts a transition from girlhood to womanhood.

While this is a book about selfhood, I hope it is not overly self-involved. I have attempted to look at the same things anew—the same rooms, the same roads—and to work out fresh ways of seeing. To tell the truth but tell it slant, to paraphrase Dickinson. Ultimately, *Soap* is a constellation of quiet truths.

Acknowledgements

Poems in this collection have been published in *Griffith Review, Westerly, Overland, Verity La, Axon: Creative Explorations, Cordite, Voiceworks, Grieve: Stories and poems for grief awareness, volume 5* and *Writ Poetry Review*.

I could not have written *Soap* without the mentorship of Paul Hetherington. It simply wouldn't have happened, and for all his time, patience and encouragement I am so grateful.

Shane Strange at Recent Work Press has been equally instrumental in bringing this collection into being. Shane has made this first-book experience a smooth and enjoyable one, and I am proud to be among such great company at Recent Work.

To Terri-ann White: thank you for always making time to read my writing, and for encouraging me to think seriously about what and why I write.

Thank you also to the Katharine Susannah Prichard Writers Centre who granted me a residency in 2015, and to Caitlin Maling, who provided me with valuable feedback on an early version of this manuscript. Thanks must also go to Lucy Dougan and Emily Stewart; and to my friend and fellow poet Alexis Lateef for always treating my writing with such respect.

And to my parents and friends who champion my work with such warmth: thank you.

2016 Editions

Pulse **Prose Poetry Project**
Incantations **Subhash Jaireth**
Transit **Niloofar Fanaiyan**
Gallery of Antique Art **Paul Hetherington**
Sentences from the Archive **Jen Webb**
River's Edge **Owen Bullock**

2017 Editions

A Song, the World to Come **Miranda Lello**
Cities: Ten Poets, Ten Cities **Various**
The Bulmer Murder **Paul Munden**
Dew and Broken Glass **Penny Drysdale**
Members Only **Melinda Smith and Caren Florance**
the future, un-imagine **Angela Gardner and Caren Florance**
Proof **Maggie Shapley**
Black Tulips **Moya Pacey**
Soap **Charlotte Guest**
Isolator **Monica Carroll**
Ikaros **Paul Hetherington**
Work & Play **Owen Bullock**

all titles available from
www.recentworkpress.com

www.ingramcontent.com/pod-product-compliance
Lightning Source LLC
Chambersburg PA
CBHW032052290426
44110CB00012B/1056